Presenting With Pizzazz

Terrific Tips For Topnotch Trainers

by

Sharon L. Bowman, M.A.

More about
Sharon Bowman,
author, NSA member,
and trainer of trainers:

• • • • •

"NSA Gateway Chapter members got so involved with exercises designed to connect audience members that we had to be bounced from the training site an hour after the program ended. As part of her "Breaking the Mold" workshop, Sharon Bowman showed us dozens of exercises that help audiences feel comfortable and involved. Larry Baker, 15-year NSA veteran, said the program 'had the highest content of any NSA event I've attended. Ever.'"

Elaine Floyd
Editor, NSA Gateway Chapter Newsletter:
"Saint Louis Speaks"

• • • • •

"Exactly what I needed to make the move from being a good trainer to being an effective, motivational, and organized trainer/facilitator ... my training has taken on new life!"

Marti Finn
Coordinator of Training Services
Private Industry Council Job Center,
Evansville, IN

• • • • •

"I had really been struggling with ways to make the drier parts of my program more fun - both for participants and for myself - and I came home (from Sharon's session) with so many ideas I couldn't get to sleep for hours!"

Nancy Rice
NSA Member, Owner
First Impressions, MO

"Informative, energizing and inspirational ... Sharon's positive outlook is contagious and our seminar attendees have caught it!"

Ralph A. Kraus,
Director of Programs OMTI
Professional Development Services, OH

• • • • •

"Sharon's pizzazz-filled workshops combine practical ideas, humor, and motivation to produce the highest impact for participants regardless of their learning styles."

Curt Hansen
Training Coordinator
Michigan Works!

• • • • •

"Sharon has the three crucial qualities of a great training designer/facilitator: total confidence in her ability to help people learn, a deep understanding of how adults take in information, and incredible creativity."

Carolyn Thompson
President, Training Systems, IL

• • • • •

"I have had multiple opportunities to use (Sharon's techniques) in one-on-one communication challenges, training and staff meetings ... the most constructive and immediately applicable material I ever learned."

Vickie Byrd
Vice-President of Operations
Career Resources, IN

• • • • •

"Sharon Bowman is deeply knowledgeable about training and teaching techniques ... and we had the most fun! I even ended up rolling on the floor laugh-

ing at the end of one session! She's the most masterful trainer I've ever known."

Cindee Davis
Instructor and Trainer
Truckee Meadows Community College, NV

• • • • •

"The books I have read and presentations attended involving audience rapport and involvement have paled in impact after attending only a two-hour session with Sharon Bowman!"

Dr. Larry D. Baker, CSP
St. Louis, MO

• • • • •

"I've trained or brokered nationally-known trainers for more than 15,000 people. Since experiencing Sharon Bowman, a new standard has been set. She is, indisputably, the best!"

Joyce Duvall, President
The Duvall Center, Inc., IN
"Where People and Organizations Grow"

Terrific Tips For Topnotch Trainers

by

Sharon L. Bowman, M.A.

**Copyright ©1997 Sharon L. Bowman, M.A.
All rights reserved.**

Published by: **Bowperson Publishing Co.**
P.O. Box 564, Glenbrook, NV 89413
775-749-5247

Fourth printing June 2002

Cover design and text layout by:
Ad Graphics, Inc., Tulsa, OK 800-368-6196

Printed in the United States of America.

Library of Congress
Catalog Card Number: 97-92966

ISBN 0-9656851-0-1

Special thanks to:

• • • • •

My boyfriend **Ross Barnett** who was there growling encouragements through the whole book birthing; my new author/speaker friend **Joanna Slan** who turned me on to the Larry Winget "stuff" and said I could do it too; my soul-sister **Jan Thurman** who helped the Corn-Row Woman to grow and the Goddess of the Stars to laugh; my longtime training partner and buddy **Joyce Duvall** who cheered on the little blooming peony; her husband **Gene Critchfield** for his peaceful spirit; creatively crazy **Curt Hansen** whose high energy is a shot-in-the-arm; my soul-brother **Ron Bush** whose prayers I count on; the topsy-turvy e-mail queen **Cindee Davis**; the little dancin' sparkle **Glenda Tedford**; and last but in no way least (how could she be? she's the reason I'm here today!) my **Mom, Frances Eleanor Patricia Jeanne Ronan Bowman** (her name is longer than her age), for her pride in her "author-trainer" daughter.

Editing and contributions by:

Ross Barnett
Frances Bowman
Cindee Davis
Joyce Duvall
Curt Hansen
Joanna Slan
Glenda Tedford
and many other friends

Permission to quote and reference organizations:

• • • • •

Bob Pike, President
Creative Training Techniques International,Inc.
(copyright quotation from:
*Creative Training Techniques Handbook,
Second Edition.*)

David Meier, President
The Center for Accelerated Learning

This book is dedicated to

COLLEEN HOSMAN,

*my angel friend,
whose interpretation
of the baby monkey dream
gave birth to this book,
and whose spiritual support
has become my lifeline.*

*W*hatever you can do,
or dream you can,
begin it!
Boldness has genius
and power and magic
in it!

...Goethe

Contents

• • • • •

Introduction

• • • • •

Are you a trainer, presenter, teacher, speaker, lecturer, facilitator - in other words, *a giver of information?* This book is for you!

Do you give information to audiences, trainees, participants, learners, students, colleagues, staff - in other words, *the receivers of information?* This book is for you!

Are you involved in doing or creating trainings, presentations, seminars, workshops, classes, lessons, speeches, lectures, learning experiences - in other words, *situations where learning is taking place?* This book is for you!

> *The training tips in this book apply to any situation where there is a giving and receiving of information.*

These tips are remarkable in their simplicity and revolutionary in their approach to teaching and learning. When you use the ideas in this book, you will be experimenting with "cutting-edge learning technology." Put another way, *you'll be creating learning experiences for your audiences and trainees that will be unforgettably unique, fun, and productive at the same time.* In addition, many of the ideas can be adapted to more intimate learning situations - like when you're explaining something to your child, spouse, or significant other, when you're working with colleagues or clients, whenever and wherever there is an exchange of information.

If you are currently in the training field, the training tips and activities were especially created with you in mind. Whether you do one-hour keynote addresses or three-day workshops, whether you are on-the-road or belong to the training department of an organization, whether you do motivational or technical training, **you'll find these training tips wonderfully creative and useful.**

When you've finished reading this book, and you've been practicing the training tips until they become part of your own artistry and magic as a trainer, presenter, or giver of information, perhaps one day you'll have an experience similar to the following. You'll be standing wearily in a long check-out line in your local grocery store and a total stranger will walk up to you and say excitedly, "I heard you speak ten years ago. You were wonderful! I remember everything you said." And then the stranger will list in vivid and endless detail all he learned from you. It'll put you on a training high for a long time!

Pop Quiz!

Pop Quiz!

• • • • •

H ave you ever heard a very funny stand-up comedian who kept you laughing for an hour?
And then the next day, when you're telling your
friends at work all about the show and they ask
you to repeat some of the jokes and one-liners, you
remember maybe two or three? And you say, "I
can't remember most of the jokes, but they sure
were funny."

Or how about a great keynote speaker, one who
keeps you thinking and chuckling for the better part
of forty-five minutes? Yet when asked later what
the speaker said, you reply, "I don't really remember the details but she spoke about organizational
change - and she was really great."

Maybe there have been times when you've explained
something to your son or daughter for the fiftieth
time and complained in exasperation, "Didn't you
hear what I just said? Why can't you remember to
do it? Why do I have to keep reminding you?"

Whoosh ... instead of reading this book, imagine
that you've been suddenly transported, without your
knowledge or consent, to an old, musty classroom,
chalk-dust hanging in the air, heavy wooden desks
screwed to the floor. Scrawled across the scratched
blackboard are the words: "Pop Quiz!" You grab a
pencil and answer the following questions quickly
by circling one of the percentages (you don't have
much time and you want out of there fast):

1. We remember how much of what we read?
   Circle one:
   10%   **50%**   **100%** *(you know better than that!)*

2. We remember how much of what we hear?
   20%   **40%**   **60%** *(say what?)*

3. We remember how much of what we see?
   10%   **30%**   **50%**

4. We remember how much of what we see and hear?
   30%   **50%**   **70%** *(think of television)*

5. We remember how much of what we say?
   40%   **60%**   **80%**

6. We remember how much of what we say and do?
   50%   **70%**   **90%**

Guess what? You get to check your own pop quiz answers. You even get to give yourself your own grade. Oh, the joys of modern education!

Aha ... the RIGHT answers:

1. We remember 10% of what we read;

2. We remember 20% of what we hear;

3. We remember 30% of what we see;

4. We remember 50% of what we see and hear;
(Ever watch a television rerun and think, "Wow! I don't even remember that scene. How could I have forgotten that part?")

5. We remember 80% of what we say;

6. We remember 90% of what we say and do.

If you got an A, or close to it, give yourself a pat on

the back. If you got an F, all you need to remember is this:

> ### It doesn't really matter what you know. It's what you do with what you know that's important.

That little fact will make you feel a lot better. And it's true! The statistics mean nothing until you start applying them to what you do, That's what this fabulous little book is all about:

Helping you give it so they get it!

In a nutshell, most of us will never have total recall but **when we say and do something we up the odds considerably** (I'll take 90% odds in my favor any day!). Unfortunately, after reading this you will remember only 10% of it, but if you tell someone about it and use the information in your next presentation, you will begin remembering more and more of it until *YOU TOO* will be considered a terrific training expert - or at least a great giver of information!

Back to our stand-up comedian and great keynote speaker. We do love to laugh. Humor is a wonderful endorphin release - and all those happy chemicals runnin' around footloose and fancy free in your body make you feel good. The funny stories humorists tell also paint amusing pictures in your head - and you remember 30% of what you see even if it's only in your head. **The downside is that you'll probably still forget 70% of the stories even if they're knee-slappin' funny.** Unless you have a strong auditory memory you'll remember how entertaining the comedian was but won't remember the specific jokes ("Yeah, he told one about his dog, but I forget the punch line"). How do you know if your memory for the spoken word is really strong? Can someone give you verbal directions to their house for the first time and you remember them without having to write them down or create a mental map of them? If so, you're probably one of those remarkable people who can remember lots more than 20% of what you hear and you've been wondering all this time what's wrong with everyone else.

Bringing it closer to home, think about all those frustrating times in which you have endlessly repeated instructions to your kids, spouse, friends, or colleagues. In all probability, they forgot close to 80% of what you said. **It didn't matter if you said it over and over, louder and louder - they still forgot it!**

There is an absolutely profound point to all this and it has to do with you as a giver of information. Here it is:

If you want them to HEAR it, YOU talk.
If you want them to LEARN it, THEY talk.

It's that simple, my friend. It doesn't matter if you're giving information to your nine year old, to your significant other, to your staff, to a group of forty trainees, or to a key-note audience of two hundred, **do you want them to HEAR it or do you want them to LEARN it?**

More importantly, do *I* want *YOU* to hear it or to learn it? Since you'll only remember 10% of what you read in this little book, I want you to say and do things with the information you read so that *YOU* will learn it too.

Your Turn...

⋙ Now, quickly, close your eyes and think of the most important point of this introduction so far. Now open your eyes, turn to your houseplant (or coffee cup, tv screen, pet, or favorite picture) and tell it what that important point was.

⋙ On a blank page in this book scribble (it's okay to scribble and doodle in books!) a word or phrase that describes what you just learned. Now add a doodle drawing to the scribble that creates a picture of what you just read. Find someone alive in your home and explain your drawing to her (or him). If she laughs, that's good! It's her endorphin release for the day and she'll be a happier person to be around.

⋙ On a sticky post-it note, write the following:

> **If I want them to HEAR it,**
> **I talk;**
> **If I want them to LEARN it,**
> **they talk.**

Stick the note to your bathroom mirror or office desk where you'll read it everyday until the sticky stuff wears off and it falls into the circular file.

Tip #1:
Never Talk Longer Than The Average Age Of The Group.

Tip #1:
Never Talk Longer Than The Average Age Of The Group.

• • • • •

You're probably wondering, "Now just what exactly does that mean?" If you're talking to a group of AARP members, does it mean you speak for seventy minutes? Or to a group of corporate executives for forty minutes? Do you ask each person his age, entering the figures on a pocket calculator to do the mathematical averaging?

Nope! It simply means when you're talking to your five year old, you speak only five minutes. If it's your teenager, fifteen minutes is maximum (sometimes you have to go back to the five minute mark). *And if you're speaking to an adult audience, 20 - 30 minutes of lecture is the ballpark figure.*

Picture this: You stand in front of your audience, look intently at them, and announce,"I need to let you know that I never talk longer than the average age of the group." Immediately you slowly and thoughtfully scan the group as if you're figuring out their average age in your head. Finally you nod wisely and observe, "Yes, just as I thought. About twenty to twenty-five years old is the average age in this room so I promise you I won't speak longer than 20 - 30 minutes at a time." They'll chuckle (unless they really are only 20 - 25 years old!) and they'll also be very interested to see whether or not you can actually do what you say you're going to do. After all, many presenters love to hear the sound of their own voice and find it painful to be quiet after only thirty minutes.

I'll let you in on a little secret: it doesn't mean that you stop speaking entirely for the rest of the time.

It just means that you stop for a few moments and let your audience DO SOMETHING with what you just told them.

I know, you're protesting, "I've got an hour to give them all this information and she wants me to stop after twenty minutes and have them *do something?* What a waste of my time!" Hang in there and hear me out.

After thirty minutes of scintillating lecture, you stop talking and say,

"My time is up. Now it's your turn to talk. Turn to the person sitting next to you and tell him three things you just learned in the last thirty minutes."

Give them about 30 - 60 seconds to repeat what they learned and then go on with the presentation. Or you can say,

"On scratch paper, or on the back of your agenda page, draw a doodle representing the most impor- tant point you just heard. Now explain your doodle drawing to the person sitting next to you."

The point is to break up your lecture/presentation/

speech with short quick **little doings**, called **Pair Shares,** so that your audience gets a chance to review the information in small chunks. It's worth repeating here: **they'll only remember 20% of what you say when they just hear it alone, but they'll remember at least 80% of what you say when they get a chance to repeat it.** A nice jump in memory there! The added bonus is: you are keeping them awake by keeping them on their toes - literally and figuratively - every thirty minutes.

Pair Share #1: "Turn to your neighbor - the person sitting next to you - and tell him three things you just learned in the last thirty minutes."

Pair Share #2: "On scratch paper, or on the back of your agenda page, draw a doodle representing the most important point you just heard. Now explain your doodle drawing to your neighbor."

Pair Share #3: "Turn to the person sitting behind you (across from you, next to you, etc.) and tell that person what you feel was the most important point of the information you heard."

Pair Share #4: "Stand up, turn to your neighbor (I always tell them to make sure no one is left out; they can also form standing triads) and tell this person two pieces of information you think you can use from the lecture."

Pair Share #5: "Think of a motion that could represent what you just learned. Now stand up and show your neighbor the motion and explain it to him." (This serves two purposes: people begin to think in "metaphors," i.e. representing one thing with a different thing - a powerful way of locking in information - and it gets their bodies moving and active so that they stay awake longer.)

Pair Share #6: "If you had to represent what you have just learned with a sound, what would the sound be? Turn to your neighbor and tell him the sound and why you chose it."

Pair Share #7: "Think of one way you could use the information you have learned so far. Stand up, find a person standing across the room from you, introduce yourself, and tell that person how you could use this information."

Pair Share #8: "Turn to the person behind you and ask him a *Pop Quiz* question about what has been presented so far. Make sure that you know the answer to the question."

Pair Share #9: "If you had to represent this information with an animal (a car, a color, a movie title, a household gadget, etc.) what animal would you choose and why? Tell your neighbor." (Again, these are metaphors for the learning - a little wacky and definitely fun.)

Pair Share #10: "If your life depended upon remembering what you just heard, how would you explain it to your executioner? Tell the person sitting in front of you."

Pair Share #11: "Stand up, move around the room, and tell three other people three different things you remember about what you just learned."

Pair Share #12: "Write one word that captures the essence of what you just learned. Now show your word to at least five other people in the room."

You see how easy it is? The **Pair Shares** are short, sweet, absolutely content related, and they help your audience review and remember the information you've presented. Besides that, the activities are fun and they keep people awake and alert, something that is oftentimes hard to do after sitting in one place for thirty minutes. So give it a try. One little **Pair Share** every thirty minutes is a good start. You can do them more often if you're brave enough - and your audience will love you for it.

Your Turn...

〰 Let's see how much you've learned. Go stand in front of a mirror - *NOW*. Look at yourself, smile, and tell yourself out loud three new ideas you got from this chapter - ideas that you would be willing to use in your next presentation.

〰 Dig up the outline of one of your presentations, workshops, speeches, anything! Now make some notes in the margins of the outline of **Pair Shares** you could use and where you would put them in your presentation.

〰 Verbally rehearse the short instructions for three **Pair Shares** until you're really comfortable explaining them to an audience.

〰 **Go out and give it a try. You'll be fabulous!**

Tip #2:
The Person Doing The Most Talking Is Doing The Most Learning.

Tip #2:
The Person Doing The Most Talking Is Doing The Most Learning.

•••••

Y ou already know this! Why am I repeating it? Because, if you're talking for thirty minutes, and you have your audience talk for one minute, then you talk again for another thirty minutes,

YOU are still doing the most learning!

Whenever you're doing the talking - or moving or writing - you're mastering what you're talking about. It's not until your training participants get to talk - and move and write - that they begin to master it too.

Have you ever noticed that, when some trainers think their training participants aren't "getting it," they repeat "it" again? They may also write it while repeating it. Now I ask you: who's doing the learning? Instead, what if a trainer had his participants repeat it and write it and teach it to someone else in the room? *Who would be doing the learning then?*

Of course, all the little **Pair Shares** will help you spread the learning around. When it comes to audience involvement, ideas abound!

Van and Vanna Volunteers: Whenever possible, have someone from your audience do your writing for you - on charts, overhead transparencies, anytime you want something recorded, and especially when you're listing the group's responses. This gives the group ownership of the information, puts everyone on alert that they might be the next "Van" or "Vanna," and guarantees that at least one person (the one doing the writing) is doing the most learning. Be sure to have the group applaud the volunteer afterwards. And if something is misspelled (like the word "misspelled" - is it or isn't it? - only old Webster knows for sure!) you can always say, "I have the highest respect for a person who can spell a word more than one way!"

Writing Rotation: Rotate the writing job among the participants. Or have two people write at the same time on two separate charts. This works especially well if you are recording group responses. The two writers can alternate the participants' words so they can keep up with the flow of the comments.

Note-Taking: Have your trainees take notes. Writing is a doing thing, and most people can remember more of what *THEY* write than what *YOU* write. By the way, notes can be doodles, a word or phrase, a mind-map (also called clustering, brainstorming, fish-boning, and bubbling). You can provide them with a fun, high-energy, cartoon-riddled, note-taking handout where they can scribble and doodle to their heart's content. Throw in a bunch of "smelly" felt tip markers to use (you know the ones that have the smells with the colors - strawberry for red, licorice for black), and people will be in kid-heaven! In addition, there's a brain-based reason for using smelly markers: olfactory sensations are registered in the emotional ("limbic") part of the brain and can play a strong part in remembering things, *like the information you're presenting.* A gentleman in one of my workshops enjoyed the smells so much he unknowingly painted his mustache purple by passing the marker under his nose a few times! Talk about an endorphin release for the rest of us!

Homeplay: Assign homeplay to be done after the presentation (one woman came up to me at a break and said, "I don't care what you call it - it's still homework!"). The homeplay is simple: "Tonight at home, get on the phone with a friend or teach one member of your family three things you learned from this workshop and how you're going to use those three things in your own life."

Play Break: Do homeplay at a break where participants take one minute to tell someone else what they learned and how they are going to use it.

Wait Time: If you ask a question, be sure to wait at least a slow five seconds (more if you can stomach the silence) before speaking again. That will give your training participants time to think about it and respond. Too often we ask questions only to jump in two seconds later with the answers. The message then becomes, "I really don't care to hear your answer because I have the right one." Not the best message to give.

Coaching: If there are real-life, physical skills involved in what they have learned, include a practice time in the training where participants coach each other through the skills.

A Final Note: If you find it hard to move off center stage (often we don't realize how long we've been talking once we're in front of a group), have a friend or new acquaintance in the audience throw you a high-sign when your thirty minutes is up. ***That will be the signal for you to stop talking and let your trainees do some talking or moving or writing.*** The sacrifice is worth it.

Your Turn...

〜 If you were held captive in your chair, bound in chains and duct tape, and had to repeat three ideas you got from this chapter before your captors would release you, what would you say?

〜 Write yourself a commitment letter:

> **"Dear** (your name):
>
> ***During my next presentation, I promise I'll do the following:*** (include one or two activities that will get your participants talking instead of you). ***It'll be exciting and enjoyable to watch my audience get into the act.***
>
> **Commitedly yours,** (your name)."

〜 Jot yourself some bright post-it note reminders during your next training - reminders like: ***"Let THEM write it. Let THEM say it. Let THEM answer it. Let THEM do it."*** Stick the reminders to the podium, the overhead, the microphone, your clothes, or some portion of your anatomy.

Tip #3:
Tell It With
Stories.

Tip #3:
Tell It With Stories.

• • • • •

Remember the children's stories your folks would read to you before bed? How about the parables in the Bible? Know someone who is so entertaining that you could listen to her stories for hours and not get bored? (I'm not saying that you'd remember them all though.) A story is a powerful way of illustrating a particular point because it paints a mental picture and that, as you know, jumps the learning to at least 30% of what is heard. In fact, if you want to get picky about it, a story is both seeing (inside your head) and hearing (outside your head) so the remembering factor could be as high as 50% - just like television.

I learned two crucial points about story-telling from celebrated author and speaker Joanna Slan. The first is: *your story needs to be your own.* When you speak from your own experience, you speak with passion and the story carries more fire and feeling. According to Joanna, many of us overlook the stories in our own lives because we are too focused on the high drama of the news media and world events. The truth is when we shift our focus to the myriad of little stories that make up our daily lives, we then dip into a larger pool of human experience.

> **"What is most personal is most universal."**

(If the author of that quote would please raise his hand, I would be happy to give him or her the credit. I heard it from Joanna who heard it from someone else who heard it - well, you get the picture.)

The second crucial point is: *if you do quote someone else's story be sure to give that person full credit for it - always!* All too often your audience has heard the quoted story and they know where it came from. *It really is wiser - and a much better learning experience - to use your own stories from your own life experiences.*

Stories don't need to be funny, they just need to be real. And they need to be relevant to the information being given. Telling a story for the sake of the story leaves people with the thought: "What did that have to do with the price of rice in China?" Unless, of course, you announce beforehand that you're going to take a little verbal "birdwalk" which is another way of saying that you're going to stray from the topic at hand for a bit.

By the way, Joanna has one final hint: "Go ahead and ham your stories up. Using your voice, your body, and your face as instruments to tell the stories will help keep your audiences entertained." *More importantly, your audiences will remember your stories - and the important information you're illustrating - far longer with a little dramatization.*

Remember that your participants have some very funny topic-related stories of their own to tell. If you give them a chance to share their own experiences, quite often they will be hilarious (the stories, I mean). *If story-telling is difficult for you, then include time for the participants to become*

the story-tellers. You're off the hook, they feel honored, and the room will fill with happy endorphins.

Your Turn...

〜〜 Take a moment now to think of a few interesting, crazy, poignant, or funny things that have happened in your life.

〜〜 Jot those stories down. Add a few vivid details to make them come alive (sights, sounds, smells, tastes, touches, colors, textures, anything to link them more strongly to the physical senses of your listeners).

〜〜 Brainstorm the training categories those stories could illustrate like change, stress, communication, money, family, etc. ***How many different ways could you use your stories? How many different points could you make with them?***

〜〜 Share your stories with your training buddies. Practice telling your stories to them. Ask for suggestions and feedback.

〜〜 Make a collection of your own stories - you'll be surprised how rich your own life has been.

Tip #4:
Balance Active And Passive Ways Of Learning.

Tip #4:
Balance Active
And Passive
Ways Of Learning.

· · · · ·

When I first learned how to include **Pair Shares** in my presentations and trainings, I went a bit overboard with active participation. I know now that one **Pair Share** every five minutes was somewhat excessive! What I've learned to do since is to balance an active "doing" with a more quiet "thinking" activity. In other words, if my training participants have done a "stand-up-move-around-getting connected" activity, the next one may be a "turn-to-your-neighbor-and-discuss" activity. Or, if I first direct a neighborly discussion, the next activity might be a "think-and-write-down" experience, called a **Personal Reflection.**

> **Variety is the spice of life,
> the name of the game,
> and crucial to successful learning.**

There are really sound physiological reasons for balancing active and passive ways of learning. First, you're actually engaging both sides of the "thinking brain" (called cerebral hemispheres) when you use a variety of activities. This means the learning has more of a chance to "stick" when the whole brain is being consciously exercised.

A second reason for making sure you have both active and passive learning experiences in your presentation has to do with what I call the "secretary" in your brain.

Have you ever driven from home to work on your regular route - and had no idea how you got there? You don't remember anything about the drive other than the fact that you made it? Have you ever been in a room with a steady noise, say a clock chiming the quarter hours, and at first the noise drives you crazy but after about two hours you don't even hear it? You would swear the clock had broken.

Inside your head is a special part of the brain responsible for deciding what sensory input gets through and what doesn't. The "secretary" sits in the office between the emotional (limbic) and the thinking (cerebrum) brains and decides who or what gets to have the attention of the thinking brain. It is the secretary (also called the "recticular activating system") that says, "Been there, done that. You don't have to pay attention on this drive to work - I can handle it. Feel free to take a mental hike for a while." If something different were to happen on the drive, say a car suddenly pulled out in front of you, the secretary would sound the alarm and the thinking brain would wake up with a start!

What does all this have to do with active and passive ways of learning?

> **Every time you vary an activity**
> **you wake up the secretary**
> **who alerts the thinking brain**
> **to pay attention.**

When your presentation participants settle in their chairs for a long sit while they listen to you, the secretary again drones, "Been there, done that. No need to pay attention now. I'll let you know when." Throw in an active **Pair Share** here and a more passive **Personal Reflection** there and the secretary keeps repeating, "Whoops - gotta pay attention! Haven't done this before. Here comes another one. Heads up!"

Personal Reflection #1: "Write three things you just learned. Now put a colored dot (star, checkmark, sticker) beside the one that is the most important of the three."

Personal Reflection #2: "Write one sentence explaining what you just heard in the last thirty minutes."

Personal Reflection #3: "Draw a face that represents how you feel about this information. Now write a sentence explaining what the face represents."

Personal Reflection #4: "On a scratch paper, write a question you still have about the information presented. Give it to me at the break."

Personal Reflection #5: "On one post-it note write a *WOW* - something you learned that was important to you. On another post-it note write a *HOW-ABOUT?* - something you still have a question about or something you want covered in the training. Now post the notes on the two charts." (Have two easily accessible chart pages taped to the walls labeled *"WOW!"* and *"HOW ABOUT?"*)

Personal Reflection #6: "Write three ways you could use the information you just learned. Circle the one you plan to do tomorrow."

Personal Reflection #7: "Spend the next four minutes reading and reviewing the information in your packet (handout, book, worksheet), and highlight the important points. In the margins, jot down any questions you still have."

Personal Reflection #8: "As you read and review the written information, draw doodles in the margins that will help you remember what you read."

Bonus Tip: "Energy" Is The Name Of The Game.

Learn to sense the ebb and flow of group energy so that you can create a balance of high, medium, and low energy activities during your presentation. Have a **Trainer's Toolbox** of activities at your disposal for changing the group energy when necessary. For example, use an **Energizer** when the group is tired, do a quiet calming activity to help people refocus after a high energy activity, call for a stretch break when needed. You can also elicit the help of the group in letting you know what they need.

Energizer #1: Micro and Macro Stretches

The group forms a standing circle. Each person in the circle takes a turn at directing the group to do a micro stretch (moving small body parts like fingers, toes, eyebrows, etc.) or a macro stretch (moving large body parts like arms, legs, torso, etc.) The group does each stretch being demonstrated (about 5 seconds per stretch).

Energizer #2: Musical Mingle

You need to have an odd number of people for this activity - you can join in to make the odd person each time. Direct the group to move around the room and stretch in time to the upbeat music you are playing. When the music stops, each person must pair up with someone else to form a standing pair. The person left out sits down but before moving can take with him anyone he can reach out and touch from where he is standing. There must be an odd number of people standing to repeat the activity. Repeat the procedure a few times until most of the participants are seated.

Energizer #3: Movin' Madness

The group forms a standing circle. While upbeat music plays, each person takes a turn standing in the middle of the circle and creating a movement symbolizing how they are feeling at the moment (about 5 seconds per person).

Energizer #4: Face-to-Face

You need to have an even number of people to start this activity. Then, when you jump in the game after the first round, there will be an odd number. Direct the group to form standing pairs. Tell them they will need to touch body part to body part until you say switch at which point they must find a new partner. You start by saying, "Face-to-face (wait). Back-to-back (wait). Side-to-side. Elbow-to-elbow. Toe-to-toe. Switch!" You then jump in the game and get a partner. The person left without a partner will be the new "caller." This person says the body-part to body-part and tells the group to switch after a few calls. This person needs to jump back into the game so that a new non-paired person gets to be the caller. Repeat the procedure a few times.

Your Turn...

〜 Can you remember an active **Pair Share** and a passive **Personal Reflection** activity? See if you can repeat the names and instructions for both without looking at the descriptions. If not, then read and rehearse one of each until you are comfortable with them.

〜 Call a training buddy on the phone and tell him about a **Pair Share** and a **Personal Reflection** activity. See if your friend has other ideas you can use.

〜 Create a **Trainer's Toolbox,** a collection of all sorts of useful, fun, creative, and successful training activity ideas. Your collection can be a colorful box where you stuff all the ideas written on scraps of paper, an organized and very official-looking binder, a file-folder, a ball with ideas pasted or written on it, a bulletin board collage, or any combination of places to put ideas.

〜 Make a list of a few active and passive learning activities you would be comfortable including in your next presentation. Circle the ones you promise yourself to use.

〜 Try the following to see what this kind of a balance feels like. Get up, move around, **do something physical now!** Then sit back down, breathe quietly, and read, write, compute, whatever. Do this a number of times during the day. Notice the effect this balance has on your body. And notice too how it keeps your brain alert and your energy level up - besides being a pretty healthy way to spend your day.

Tip #5:
Walk Your
Talk.

Tip #5:
Walk Your Talk.

• • • • •

I once attended a workshop where the trainer spoke for an hour about how adults needed active learning experiences. My mind was screaming, "Then let us *DO* something, for pete's sake!" Fortunately my mouth remained closed. Or, in hindsight, maybe it wasn't so fortunate. I know I was not the only person in the room who desperately needed some active learning experiences *right then.*

A friend of mine attended a five-day train-the-trainer course. The first day was about "making connections" and creating a "learning community." Unfortunately, the trainer's idea of making connections was to have everyone listen to her stories and connect with her, not with the other participants. The group never really formed the learning community they were studying. When it came time for them to hand out certificates on the last day, they were each given someone else's certificate and told to say something nice about the person as they gave him/her the certificate. Almost without exception, each person struggled with something to say because they didn't know each other well enough to be able to say anything. *They spent five days together and still didn't know each other.* Sad.

> **Don't preach about something you aren't willing to do yourself or haven't yet practiced.**

Speak from your own experiences. Be up front about whether or not you have used what you're talking about. And above all, have your participants practice the skills you're giving them. Bob Pike, president of Creative Training Techniques International, Inc., has a great line: "Fu Yu, Wu Yu, Wzu Tu Yu." Roughly translated it means: "Mama's havin' it and Papa's havin' it ain't like baby havin' it!" Another way to put it is:

Talkin' 'bout it ain't the same as doin' it!

If you're preachin', then you'd better be practicin' - and havin' them practice as well!

Bonus Tip:
Who You Are Speaks Louder
Than What You Say.

Your energy and your non-verbal communication are more powerful training tools than the content of your presentation. Be aware and learn to consciously use eye contact, gestures, movement, different voice tones, verbal pacing, facial expressions, and dramatization to keep your audience interested and awake. **Step out of your comfort zone and take some risks with new presentation techniques.** You'll feel excited and energized - and so will your audience.

Your Turn...

〜 **Pop-quiz!** What does "Fu Yu, Wu Yu, Wzu Tu Yu" mean? What does it have to do with *YOU* as a giver of information? **Say your thoughts out loud or write them down.**

〰 Ask a trusted friend to attend one of your presentations and give you constructive feedback about your non-verbal communication. Your friend can also kindly draw your attention to words or gestures that you repeat a lot (we all do that unknowingly).

〰 **"A picture is worth a thousand words."** If you're really brave, have a friend or colleague videotape you rehearsing or actually giving your presentation. When you sit down to watch the videotape, pretend that you're part of the audience and the person presenting is a stranger to you. What things do you notice? How would you react to this presenter? What are some kudos and suggestions you would want to give her? (I have to say in all honesty that I still can't do this. I have great difficulty being that objective when I'm up there on that television screen. I don't know how actors do it.)

〰 Be particularly honest with yourself when looking at the information you are giving and decide if you are truly "walking your talk" or **are you just preaching stuff you've heard but not yet put into practice?** For example, in my stress management trainings one thing I *DON'T* do is tell people to exercise regularly because I'm not exercising regularly - sporadically yes, regularly no!

Tip #6:
Active
Bodies
Equal
Active
Brains.

Tip #6:
Active Bodies Equal Active Brains.

• • • • •

Have you ever attempted a physical skill as an adult - such as riding a bicycle or playing the piano - that you learned as a child and haven't done for a long time? Even though you may feel clumsy and rusty, have you noticed how different parts of your body begin to respond and move in patterns similar to the ones you knew when you were young? It's as if the knowing comes from your muscles and not your head.

> ### The body remembers
> ### what the mind may forget.

Your body will remind you of things you've forgotten. And it is through the movement of your body that your thinking brain suddenly says, "Aha ... I got it! I remember that one."

Let me give you an example. A teacher friend of mine had a son in sixth grade who was having problems in geography. The boy couldn't remember the names and locations of all the states. My friend took his son outside and drew a chalk map of the United States on the driveway. Then he had his son "walk the states" as he said each name. The boy did this a few times, each time doing it faster and faster. He aced the test - and all the geography tests after that. And he still remembers the states and their locations to this day.

David Meier, president and founder of The Center for Accelerated Learning, has a gazillion ideas for getting bodies actively involved in learning - wild and wacky ways of doing and remembering things as complicated as a nuclear power plant fusion program and as simple (oh yeah?) as remembering the parts of a computer. He even shows his trainees how they can learn to order French food in French - and remember the words years later!

Activity #1: Gallery Walk

Post chart paper sheets on the walls around the room. Depending upon what topic you're presenting, each chart paper could represent one idea, one step in a program, one skill, etc. Play some quiet "thinking" music and have participants take felt tip pens and write their own ideas on each chart. Give them about 15 seconds per chart. They can do them randomly or in a particular order. After writing, play upbeat "active" music and have your participants take a five-minute **Gallery Walk** of the room, writing down ideas on note-taking paper as they read the charts. Then have them discuss what they learned.

Activity #2: Follow the Yellow Brick Road

If your trainees are learning a specific procedure which has a number of steps to follow, have them diagram the procedure on the walls or floor using chart paper, felt pens, string, crepe paper, etc. Then they walk the procedure as they discuss and explain each step with a partner. Remember, **when they create it, they learn it.**

Activity #3: Steppin' Out

Each person in a small group represents one step of a specific procedure and acts out the step for the whole group. For example, in a job development training, a small group acted out an interviewing procedure for job seekers. Each person had a sign hanging around her neck indicating the step in the procedure and role-played that step for the class.

Activity #4: Movin' and Groovin'

Participants' bodies *actually become* the parts of whatever they are learning about. This is especially powerful in technical training. David Meier, in an Accelerated Learning workshop, had trainees become the serial and parallel ports on a computer, the bits and bytes of information, etc. They represented those parts with sounds and motions that raised the roof and the participants' spirits for the rest of the day!

Your Turn...

ᨮ Ask yourself why having an active body is so important to learning? **Now answer that question OUT LOUD.**

ᨮ What is one idea about active learning from this book that really knocks your socks off? I hope there's at least one so far! Find another person and tell him your great idea.

ᨮ Think back to some fun learning experiences you've had. What were the activities that made the learning enjoyable and productive? Jot down those ideas.

〰〰 Anytime you see/hear/experience an activity that you can use in your own trainings, add that idea to your **Trainer's Toolbox.**

Tip #7:
The Process Is
As Important
As The Product.

Tip #7:
The Process Is As Important As The Product.

. . . . .

W hat were your experiences like as a kid in school? Do you have a lot of pleasant memories or are the things that you remember unpleasant like the pain of embarrassment or fear of failure?

Here is a simple yet profound way of looking at learning:

> **You learn from pain and you learn from pleasure. Period.**

You survive and learn, no matter how painful the experience. The problem is that **when the learning has been painful** (translate as: boring, humiliating, tense, frustrating, a waste of time, etc.) **you tend to avoid any and all reminders of it later.** If you found school difficult as a kid, you'll probably not be very inclined to pursue ongoing education as an adult. Furthermore, you may almost unconsciously avoid anything that reminds you of school - like books, teachers, classrooms, libraries, etc. On the other hand, if you found school to be a pleasant and successful experience, you will most likely seek out more school-like experiences as an adult.

You carry that pain or pleasure with you into adult learning situations. And so do your trainees. They come to your presentation or training with their own learning baggage. It then becomes your job to see to it that their time spent with you is pleasant as well as productive so that *they will learn as much as they can and so that they will leave wanting more.*

> *How your participants "get there" is as important as the information they walk away with.*
> *The activities they engage in will determine the depth of the learning they leave with.*

Your greatest challenge is to create a learning experience that is pleasurable, stimulating, challenging, and informative - not too tall an order! *And you CAN do it in simple, fun, and creative ways.*

Bonus Tip: Create A Comfort Zone.

Within the limitations of the room you have in which to present, *create as comfortable and colorful a place for learning as possible.* Pay attention to lighting, sound, smell, furniture arrangement, extra clutter, seating, AV placement, colors, etc. Walk around the room to get a feel of how people standing and sitting in different locations will be able to see and work together effectively. Visualize how you want the room to look and feel, move things around, and create a setting that maximizes learning throughout the presentation. ***Especially pay attention to the little voice inside you*** that gives you subtle hints about the room: "This doesn't feel quite right. That podium looks funny there. the other side looks bare. Something needs to be moved here."

Bonus Tip:
Food Is For Thought.

If possible, request that there be beverages and "munchies" at the training. If your training is longer than one day, ask participants to bring in snacks to share the following day. The snacks can represent the learner or something they've learned. The next day each participant who brought a snack tells the group what it represents and why they chose it. Applaud the snack-bringers! Food is a nurturing thing and gives the message to your participants that ***they matter and they are worth the time, effort, and money it takes to provide nourishment.***

For many people, food is intimately connected with learning. For example, when you're studying or writing on your own at home, do you find yourself putting things in your mouth? Like sipping coffee, tea, chewing gum, munching snacks, sucking on hard candy, gnawing pencils? Food is a sensory stimulant during the learning process. Nice to know when you're pigging out on a piece of cake and reading at the same time!

Bonus Tip:
"Zen" The Room.

I observed famous educator/speaker Harry Wong do a keynote presentation for five hundred teachers. Before moving center stage, he stood quietly off to the right while the person introducing him was talking. At first he had his eyes closed, as if gathering his energy and thoughts. Then he opened his eyes and silently scanned the audience, making eye contact with a number of people and smiling at them. When he bounded to the center of the room, he had already personally connected with so many people that *I could feel the emotional shift in the room from "strangers" to "friends."*

When a trainer friend of mine makes eye contact with her trainees, she mentally recites a little mantra: *"I'm glad that you're here. I'm glad that I'm here. I know what I know."*

Before starting your presentation, *take a moment to make eye contact with as many people as possible,* welcoming them mentally as well as verbally. This little exercise is a focusing of your energy and theirs as you begin your presentation. It creates positive emotional connections. And it gives you that friendly face to return your attention to when you need a little extra support from the group.

Bonus Tip:
Connect People To People.

I lived a trainer's nightmare once - and still have the scars to prove it! I was facilitating a three-day management retreat for an agency in the Midwest. About fifteen administrators attended the training, a small and intimate number of people who knew each other well. As I discovered later, some of these people basically did not like the others and set about to "sabatoge" the group activities. "Sniping" broke out, that kind of kidding that is meant to hurt under the guise of smiles. It became so unproductive that we ended up having an intense group discussion about what was going on, and created some ground rules to use for the rest of the training.

I share that experience to illustrate the following point: **when people are not emotionally connected to each other in positive ways, the group dynamics can be destructive to learning.**

Connections are the keys to creating positive learning experiences, community building, the willingness to take risks, and the ability to open up to other people and learn from them.

> **People feeling connected to each other in positive ways is a crucial part of a successful training or presentation.**

As my example showed, if they don't get connected, and don't really like or trust each other, very little learning takes place no matter how important your information may be. **So before connecting your trainees with the content you're going to be teaching them, connect them with each other first.** Use ice-breakers, trust-building activities, energizers or anything that is fun and low-risk and that will get them up and moving and talking with each other.

Connecting Activity #1: TENS

"TENS" is an acronym for "Touch, Eyes, Name, Smile." Model doing a **TENS** with a volunteer. You stand facing the volunteer, shake hands, make eye-contact, say hi and the volunteer's name, and smile. Thank the volunteer. Then tell the participants they will have exactly 45 seconds to do a **TENS** with as many people as they can. Start the clock and join in. At the end of 45 seconds sound a noisemaker to signal stop. Make the time shorter if the group is small (under 20), or longer if it's a large group (over fifty).

Connecting Activity #2: Mingle-Mingle

Direct the group to stand. Tell them when you say "Mingle-mingle!" they are to move around the room mumbling out loud "Mingle-mingle!" When you say stop and sound a noisemaker, they are to form standing pairs or triads. Then you direct them to tell their partner the answer to the question you have on a chart or overhead transparency. Repeat this procedure two or three times. Examples of questions to discuss are:

 Why did you decide to come to this training?

 What do you already know about the training topic?

 What more do you want to learn from this training?

 What do you want to leave knowing how to do?

Or make up your own questions.

Connecting Activity #3: Birds-of-a-Feather

Tell the participants they need to find someone in the room who likes the same junk food that they do and form standing pairs. If someone hasn't found a partner (no one else likes gummy bears, for example) that person can join any pair to form a triad. Once they have a partner, direct them to introduce themselves and answer the question on a chart or overhead transparency (questions can be the same as the ones in **Mingle-Mingle** or you can make up your own). Then direct them to find a new partner, someone who has vacationed in the same place they have. Another time they find someone who drives the same make/color of car, who has a birthday in the same season, who has the same first or last name initial, who is wearing the same color, etc. Create your own **Birds-of-a-Feather.**

Your Turn...

〜 Look around the room you're in at this moment. Is there some little thing you could do to make it even more comfortable than it is? **Do it now.** Or draw a picture of the way it could be if you changed a few little things to make it more inviting.

〜 List five ways you could change the physical set-up of a training room to create a comfortable and pleasing sensory experience for your trainees.

〜 Make a promise to yourself that you're going to do a **TENS** with at least six people today. Family members and pets count too!

〜 Think back to some learning experiences you had either as a child or adult. If they were painful, what did you do afterwards so that you wouldn't have to experience the pain again? If they were pleasurable, what did you do afterwards to make the pleasure happen again? ***How does this affect you as a learner now? How about you as a presenter?***

〰 What are three things you could do to insure that the learning process is pleasant for your participants? Jot them down. Share them with a training buddy.

〰 Rehearse the instructions for one ***Connecting Activity*** until you are comfortable directing it. Get some willing friends or training buddies together who will be your local friendly guinea pigs and try out the activity on them. Be open to their helpful feedback.

Tip #8:
You Master
What You Teach.

Tip #8:
You Master What
You Teach.

• • • • •

L et's face it, you probably know your subject matter inside out. One of the reasons you're considered an expert in your chosen field is simply
because you've taught the information over and over
until you could say it in your sleep (sometimes I bet
you do!). In order for your participants to master
what they've learned, they need to do exactly what
you're doing:

> **They need to teach it
> to someone else!**

Give them opportunities to do just that.

Activity #5: Showtime

Divide your participants into small groups and have
each group present a part of the information they
learned in a creative, playful way: role-plays, demon-
strations, raps, skits, songs, pictures, pantomime,
movement, dance, etc.

Activity #6: Terrific Teachers

Have participants stand in pairs (triads are okay)

and tell them to teach the other person one skill they just learned. One person explains the skill, demonstrates it, and has the partner practice it. Then they reverse roles and repeat the process with another skill.

Activity #7: Something Old, Something New

In small groups, participants create another skill using one they've learned. They present the new skill to the group (example: during a stress managment training, participants used learned wellness techniques to create a new wellness program for all the training participants).

Activity #8: Shine On

In small groups, each participant either verbally or pictorally presents a short part of what he learned and answers questions about it.

Your Turn...

〰 Make a list of as many subject areas or skills, personally and professionally, you can think of that you have "mastered" during your lifetime. Put a happy face (OK, a check-mark) beside the ones that you've taught to others. **Think: did the teaching of it make a difference in your mastery of it? How so?**

〰 Make another list of some things you would like to teach in order to master. Can you think of a way you can begin to include bits and pieces of this list in what you're already doing?

〰 Call a training buddy and ask her what she does to make sure that her participants "master" what she's teaching. Add the ideas to your **Trainer's Toolbox.**

Tip #9:
Be The
"Guide-On-The-Side,"
Not The
"Sage-On-The-Stage."

Tip #9: Be The "Guide-On-The-Side," Not The "Sage-On-The-Stage."

• • • • •

- Are you in front of a group because you like being center stage?
- Do you love having heaps of attention focused on you?
- Perhaps putting on a show for other is a source of excitement for you?
- Maybe you get a natural high from the abundance of energy directed your way?

I'm not saying those are bad reasons for speaking to a group of people. If you said "no" to all of those questions, it's probably agonizing for you to be doing what you're doing. But if you said "yes" to all the questions, *and they're your only reasons for doing what you're doing*, then you might think about the entertainment business, not the speaking business! Come to think of it, **many trainers really are entertainers - and that's OK.** There's definitely a need and a place for it all, and for all of us.

I have a small personal bias when it comes to giving a group of people important information. ***I think*** *that it's my business as a trainer to get my train-ing participants focused on themselves and their own learning as quickly as possible.* That means I have to step off the stage because con-stantly calling attention to myself (and my gems of wit and wisdom) detracts from their work of learn-ing as much as they can.

> *I am the guide who creates*
> *the learning experience*
> *and then steps back*
> *to let the learners take over.*

It's my job to move their attention away from me and onto them. And I have to let go of my own ego enough to be able to do that. Not an easy thing to let go of! Yes, I get a high from all that positive energy directed my way. And I remind myself that the high is not the reason I'm here.

> *I'm here to help people*
> *learn some really good stuff.*
> *I'm here to help people*
> *remember the good stuff they learn*
> *long after they leave.*
> *I'm here to see to it that*
> *their learning journey with me*
> *and with each other*
> *is a positive and successful one.*

I can claim the applause when I've done all that. And you can too.

Your Turn...

ᖰ Write this profoundly important sentence on a piece of brightly-colored paper:

> **I am the guide who creates
> the learning experience
> and then steps back
> to let the learners take over.**

Post the paper where you can see it everyday. Say the words aloud each time you read it until it becomes a sort of mantra or affirmation. **Can you say it from memory? Good!**

ᖰ Think of five ways you could turn a "sage-on-the-stage" presentation to a "guide-on-the-side" one. If you haven't done it already, add them to your **Trainer's Toolbox.**

ᖰ If you're planning a keynote address or a short presentation, think of one activity you could include that would focus the learners' attention on themselves for just one or two minutes. Make yourself a promise to do that activity.

Tip #10:
"You Teach Best What You Most Need To Learn."

Tip #10:
"You Teach Best
What You Most Need
To Learn."

• • • • •

The quote is from author/speaker Richard Bach. He also reminds us:

> **"Learning is finding out
> what you already know.
> Doing is demonstrating that you know it.
> Teaching is reminding others
> that they know just as well as you."**

We are all learners, doers, and teachers!

Have you ever noticed that you often repeat the same situations and experiences? Have you asked yourself, "Why am I still doing that? Why is this still happening to me? I can't believe I'm doing it again!"

You're enrolled in a full-time informal school called "Life" and it's about repeating lessons until you learn them - and then you get new lessons to learn. **One of the most powerful ways of learning a lesson is to teach it to someone else.**

Take a look at what you're teaching. What parts of it are you still learning about? What parts of it are you still struggling with? What parts of it have you mastered? How about your participants? **What do they still need to learn and how can they teach it to one another?**

A birdwalk: Bringing it home, what is it you want your child or significant other to know? How can they teach it to you? One simple way is to ask them to show you or to have them repeat what you've said to them. You will quickly discover what has been learned and what hasn't.

Bonus Tip:
It's Okay To Say,
"I Don't Know."

You don't have to know everything about your topic. Nowhere is it written that you have to have every fact at your command before you're allowed to speak. Your audience just expects you to know a little more than they do. **They don't expect you to be the world's only expert.**

What do you say when you don't know the answer? Try:

〜 *I don't know, but I'll find out."*

〜 *"That's an interesting question. What do you think?"*

〜 *"Does anyone here have any thoughts on that issue?"*

〜 *"What do the rest of you think?"*

〰 *"Please write that question on a post-it note and put it on the chart (have a chart labeled "Parking Lot" taped to the wall where questions are "parked" for future reference) and we'll get back to it a little later."*

So you can toss a question back to the whole group. You can defer the question until a more appropriate time when you have more information. And, perhaps most importantly, **you can let your participants add to the knowledge of the group by sharing their own expertise about the topic.**

Bonus Tip:
"Feel The Fear And Do It Anyway."

You've probably been asked on numerous occasions, "Do you ever get scared of public speaking?" Every time! For me, and for many other trainers I know, the fear is always there at the beginning of a presentation, no matter how many times we've done it. **We've just learned to feel it, to move through it as quickly as possible, and to get past it to the good feelings on the other side.**

Learn what works for you during those first moments of heebie-jeebies. Take a few deep breaths, do an introductory activity that focuses participants' attention on themselves and not on you, create a mental picture that makes you smile (the book *I Can See You Naked* is a great source for more "getting-rid-of-the-training jitters" ideas) - **anything that will help you let go of any nervousness and relax into the experience as quickly as possible.** Don't tell your audience how nervous you are. They'll end up becoming nervous with you!

Your Turn...

⋙ In a nutshell, what were the training tips in this chapter about? Answer that question out loud so that you hear it too.

⋙ What do you want to learn in this lifetime that you haven't already learned? *Is there a way you could begin teaching even the little that you know about it to someone else?*

⋙ What do your friends and colleagues do to move past the fear of public speaking? If you don't know, find out.

Endings
And
Beginnings

Endings
And
Beginnings

• • • • •

F old your hands. Go ahead - fold them like you would if you were sitting with your hands folded in your lap. Now fold them *the other way!* Just slide all fingers and thumb of one hand down so the other thumb is on top. How does that feel? A little strange maybe?

Try this. Fold your arms in front of your chest. Now fold them *the other way.* You might find yourself rolling them a few times until you figure out which is the other way. How does that feel? Even stranger? Different? Wrong?

Anytime you "stretch" a bit out of your comfort zone - the way you're used to doing things - you'll feel a little uncomfortable at first. Whether it's a physical habit, a thought pattern, or a new training skill, you'll feel slightly off-kilter for a bit until the newness wears away and the habit, thought, or skill becomes your own. It'll take you about a month of practice to make something new your own, to the point where you no longer have to consciously think about what you're doing. You may not be adept at it yet but you'll feel more comfortable doing it.

Think about that when you begin to practice some

of the tips and training ideas in this book. Give yourself some "tinkering" time with the ideas, to try them out, to rework them until they fit your own presentation style. **Soon you'll be so comfortable with them that you won't remember presenting without them.** Seek out opportunities to experiment.

> ## Give yourself permission to play.

I am often asked, "What about an audience that isn't receptive to active participation? What if your participants don't want to do the activity?" In my trainings, I always give the learning rationale behind an activity and the purpose of the activity before asking my trainees to do it. I also model it for them whenever I can so that I'm the first one who may appear a bit foolish. **If it's okay for me to seem silly it'll be okay for them too.** Furthermore, I let them know that if the activity moves them too far out of their own comfort zone they can choose to "pass" and be observers. Most of the time I will get a 100% buy-in after that. If I don't, no problem. The majority of participants will join in and the ones who don't join in often take part in other activities later.

The more comfortable you are doing and directing the activities and training tips, the more comfortable your audience will be also.

> ## The more you believe in what you do, the more they will believe in it too.

There are another hundred or so training tips rattling around in my head but these will give you a good start - and will fine-tune what you're already doing well. Don't sell yourself short. You have the experience, the skills, and now some terrific training tips to be a topnotch trainer. *Go for it! You CAN present with pizzazz!*

Bonus Tip:
Celebrate The Learning!

Ever wonder why we have holidays? *To celebrate something!* Yes, to have an excuse to whoop it up and raise our glasses in a toast and shout "Congratulations!" or "Here's To Us!" or "Happy Anything!"

> *Let your trainees celebrate together their special journey with you.*

Create an ending activity that does just that. You'll want them to connect with each other again as well as with the training information so that they leave feeling good about themselves and what they've just learned. *Close your presentation with a high-energy, fun, whole group activity that celebrates the learning they experienced together.*

The activity can be as simple as a *"Koosh Throw."* Everyone stands in a circle and a koosh ball is quickly thrown randomly around the room as people share an insight they had, something they learned, a compliment to someone in the group, something they are going to do with what they learned, etc. Include in your *Trainer's Toolbox* a number of closing activities from which you can choose an appropriate one that will end the day on a high note of positive energy.

Closing Activity #1: Picture it Perfect

Each person has a blank 8 1/2 x 11 piece of paper folded into fourths. In each quadrant the participant draws a doodle representing something in the training that went well or that helped him learn. After drawing four doodles, participants walk around the room explaining their doodles to four different people.

Closing Activity #2: Car Wash

The group forms two straight lines facing each other with a space in between. The first two people at the front of the lines walk single file down the space between the lines. People in the lines give them pats-on-the-back, hand shakes, high-fives, hugs, whatever feels appropriate to do. When those two people finish going through the line, they join the end of the line on either side and the next two front-of-the-line people go through the **Car Wash** until everyone has gotten a handshake, high-five, etc.

Closing Activity #3: Reception Line

A variation of the **Car Wash** where the group forms one long line. You stand at the beginning of the line and go down the line shaking hands, giving high-fives, etc. to each person. As you do that, the next person begins, and then the next and next until you have a lot of people in the line and a lot of people moving down the line. When done, each person joins the line at the end until all have gone through the **Reception Line** once.

Closing Activity #4: Snowball Fight

Each person (including you) writes on a blank white typing page one thing he's going to do with what he's learned. Have the entire group take their papers with them and form a circle away from the furniture. Then tell them to crinkle up their papers into "snowballs." They will have about 30 seconds to hit as many people with as many snowballs as they can. You begin the **Snowball Fight** by throwing, picking up, and throwing the paper snowballs again. At the end of the time, use a noisemaker to get their attention. Ask them to pick up a snowball (it doesn't have to be their own), unfold it, and take turns reading their snowballs to the group so that everyone gets to hear all the different ideas for using the information.

Bonus Tip:
Give Yourself
A Pat On The Back.

I know I don't need to tell you that one of the greatest fears in our country is public speaking - it's listed right up there with "death, divorce, and unknown calamities!" Funny how many people can talk on and on about stuff they know when they're with a group of friends but put them in front of a group of strangers and their knees go limp.

> *You put yourself on the line and you need to acknowledge your own courage no matter how you feel the presentation turned out.*

If you are one of those trainers (and I am!) who can get thirty excellent evaluations and one poor one, and you beat yourself up over the poor one, then you need a bit of mental magic to pull yourself out of the tailspin you create. A delightful trainee told me to wave my hand as if dismissing a pesky person (she said she named the pesky person in her mind "Aunt Ninny") and say loudly and firmly, **"Besides that, Aunt Ninny, I did the best that I could."** Try it - it works!

My college instructor/trainer friend Cindee Davis suggests that an interesting shift inside your head takes place when you have a friend read aloud the excellent evaluations. **You hear them as if the writers were telling you the compliments to your face - and suddenly you believe them!** It's a great boost for your self-esteem.

Cindee also advises you to remember what you love about what you do and make a list of everything great about your work. Review the list often, especially before a presentation. As part of your preparation, create a mental picture of your best presentation and how good it felt. **Always remind yourself of the positive aspects of your past presentations** so that, instead of focusing on any mistakes, your attention is directed to the pieces that worked and your own creative artistry as a presenter. **After all, you ARE an artist.** Your palette colors are space, time, people, information, and energy. **You create the pictures, the experiences, the connections, the learning, the memories.**

You took the risks.
You made it happen.
Your participants are leaving
a little richer because of the time
they spent with you.
You did it!
Now reward yourself for doing
the best job that you could.
Go out and do something
spectacularly wonderful
for yourself!
You deserve it!

Still more about Sharon Bowman:

For those of you who need to know her credentials and experience, read the paragraphs. For those of you who want to know the interesting tidbits, read the bullets!

Sharon L. Bowman, M.A., is a Fortune 500 and workforce development trainer for business, government, and educational training programs across the United States. Sharon specializes in train-the-trainer seminars and workshops. She also offers conference sessions and interactive keynote addresses on effective communication skills, stress management, teambuilding, and learning styles.

An inveterate pro, Sharon "walks the talk" by modeling everything she teaches and by building in quality practice time for each skill to be learned. Her seminars are packed with useful and practical information, fast-paced and fun! *(Who said learning has to be boring?)*

Sharon is a member of the National Speakers Association and has been an author, educator, college faculty member, consultant and trainer for twenty-five years.

✹ She likes reading, sailing, flying a Cessna 172 (unfortunately not her own), hiking, writing, and swimming in Lake Tahoe's forty-degree waters!

✹ She dislikes liver with onions, green fuzz in the refrigerator (due to long absences from home, there's a lot of that), and intolerant people.

✹ She thinks being forty-something and in love is a heady experience!

✹ She lives in a fifty year-old stone and knotty pine "caretaker's cottage" on the Nevada shores of pristine (and cold) Lake Tahoe.

✹ She swears red hair gives her an energy boost!

✹ She welcomes thoughts, ideas, comments, stories, inspirational tidbits and cheers from her trainees and readers. Send them to:

Sharon Bowman
P.O. Box 564
Glenbrook NV 89413
Phone: 775-749-5247
Fax: 775-749-1891
E-Mail: SBowperson@aol.com
Web Site: www.Bowperson.com

You won't want to miss ...

Sharon's other great books:

How To Give It So They Get It!
A Flight Plan For Teaching Anyone Anything And Making It Stick

Shake, Rattle And Roll!
Using The Ordinary To Make Your Training Extraordinary

Preventing Death By Lecture!
Terrific Tips For Turning Listeners Into Learners

If Lazarus Did It, So Can You!
Resurrecting The Learning In Your Churches, Schools, And Homes

For ordering information log onto www.Bowperson.com or call Bowperson Publishing at 775-749-5247.

Sharon's most popular workshops:

Teach It Quick And Make It Stick!
Creating Dynamic Learning Experiences for the Adult Learner.

Help! My Job Is Driving Me Crazy!
A Fresh Look at Managing Stress.

There's More To It Than Meets The Eye!
Diversity in the Workplace.

Different Strokes For Different Folks!
Working Together Through Changing Times.

I See What You Say!
Worktalk in the Workplace.

Presenting With Pizzazz!
Creating Fun and Memorable Meetings, Presentations, and Training.

For a complete list of resources and services contact:

Sharon L. Bowman, M.A.
P.O. Box 564, Glenbrook NV 89413
Phone: 775-749-5247 • Fax: 775-749-1891
E-Mail: SBowperson@aol.com
Web Site: www.Bowperson.com

Resources

• • • • •

Some of the absolute best sources of public and in-house seminars, training resources and materials. Call for product catalogues and brochures.

The Center for Accelerated Learning
David Meier, Director
1103 Wisconsin Street, Lake Geneva, WI 53147
Phone: 262-248-7070
Fax: 262-248-1912

Creative Training Techniques: A Newsletter of Tips, Tactics and How-Tos for Delivering Effective Training.
Bob Pike, Editor
Lakewood Publications
50 S. 9th Street, Minneapolis, MN 55402
Phone: 800-328-4329
Fax: 612-340-4819

Creative Training Techniques Internl., Inc.
Robert W. Pike, CSP, President
7620 West 78th Street
Edina, MN 55439
Phone: 800-383-9210
Fax: 612-829-0260
Web Site: www.cttbobpike.com

How to Get Booked and Make Money Fast! (audio tapes)
Larry Winget: Win Seminars!
P.O. Box 700485
Tulsa, OK 74170
Phone: 800-749-4597
Fax: 918-747-3185
Web Site: www.larrywinget.com

Training Systems, Inc.
Carolyn B. Thompson, President
221 Vermont Road
Frankfort, IL 60423
Phone: 815-469-1162
Fax: 815-469-0886

CURTIS Services
Curt L. Hansen: Creativity Unlimited
5160 West Jackson Road
Elwell, MI 48832
Phone: 517-887-8410

Joanna Slan, Professional Speaker and Trainer
7 Ailanthus Court
Chesterfield, MO 63005
Phone: 800-356-2220
Fax: 314-7970

The 4MAT© System of Instructional Design
Bernice McCarthy, President
About Learning, Inc.
1251 Old Rand Road
Wauconda, IL 60084
Phone: 800-822-4628
Fax: 847-487-1811

Trainer's Warehouse
Mike Doctoroff, President
89 Washington Avenue
Natick, MA 01760
Phone: 800-299-3770
Fax: 508-651-2674

Selected Bibliography

• • • • •

*An eclectic list of some of
Sharon's favorite books.*

Bellman, Geoffrey. **The Consultant's Calling: Bringing Who You Are to What You Do.** Jossey-Bass Publishers, CA 1990

Cameron, Julia. **The Artist's Way: A Spiritual Path to Higher Creativity.** G.P. Putnam's Sons, NY 1992

Chicken Soup for the Soul at Work: 101 Stories of Courage, Compassion & Creativity in the Workplace. Health Communications, Inc. FL 1996

Chocolate for a Woman's Soul: 77 Stories to Feed Your Spirit and Warm Your Heart. Simon & Schuster, Publishers

Davidson, Jeff. **The Complete Idiot's Guide to Managing Stress.** Alpha Books, 1997

Gelb, Michael. **Present Yourself.** Jalmar Press, CA 1988

Hoff, Ron. **I Can See You Naked.** Universal Press Syndicate, KS 1992

McCarthy, Bernice. **About Learning.** Excel, Inc., IL 1996 (800-822-4628)

McGee-Cooper, Ann. **Time Management for Unmanageable People.** Bantam Books, NY 1994

Peters, Tom. **The Tom Peters Seminar: Crazy Times Call for Crazy Organizations.** Vintage Books, NY 1994

Pike, Robert W., CSP. **Creative Training Techniqes Handbook, Second Edition.** Lakewood Books, MN 1994

Rozakis, Laurie, Ph.D.
The Complete Idiot's Guide to Speaking in Public with Confidence.
Alpha Books, NY 1995

Saltzman, Joel.
If You Can Talk, You Can Write.
Warner Books, Inc. NY 1993

Samples, Bob.
Open Mind, Whole Mind.
Jalmar Press, CA 1987

Slan, Joanna.
Storytelling and Humor in Professional Speaking.
Allyn & Bacon, Publishers

Tannen, Deborah, Ph.D.
That's Not What I Meant! How Conversation Style Makes or Breaks Relationships.
Ballantine Books, NY 1986

Thompson, Carolyn.
Creating Highly Interactive Training Quickly and Effectively.
TSI Publications, IL 2000
Phone: 800-469-3560

Walsch, Neale.
Conversations with God: An Uncommon Dialogue.
G.P. Putnam's Sons, NY 1995

Where the Heart Is.
Personal Power Press, Publishers

Whyte, David.
The Heart Aroused: Poetry and the Preservation of the Soul in Corporate America.
Doubleday, NY 1994

Winget, Larry.
How to Write a Book One Page at a Time.
Win Publications, OK 1996

Williams, Linda.
Teaching for the Two-Sided Mind.
Simon and Schuster, Inc., NY 1983